It's My Body

My Neck and Shoulders

Lola M. Schaefer

Heinemann Library
Chicago, Illinois

© 2003 Heinemann Library
a division of Reed Elsevier Inc.
Chicago, IL

Customer Service 888-454-2279
Visit our website at www.heinemannlibrary.com

Designed by Sue Emerson, Heinemann Library; Page layout by Que-Net Media
Printed and bound in the United States by Lake Book Manufacturing, Inc.
Photo research by Jennifer Gillis

07 06 05 04 03
10 9 8 7 6 5 4 3 2 1

Library of Congress Cataloging-in-Publication Data
Schaefer, Lola M., 1950-
   My neck and shoulders / Lola M. Schaefer.
      v. cm. – (It's my body)
Contents: What are your neck and shoulders? – Where is your neck? – What does your neck look like? – What's inside your neck? – What can you do with your neck? – Where are your shoulders? – What do your shoulders look like? – What's inside your shoulders? – What can you do with your shoulders? – Quiz – Picture glossary.
Includes index.
   ISBN 1-4034-0892-0 (HC), 1-4034-3484-0 (Pbk.)
   1. Neck–Juvenile literature. 2. Shoulder–Juvenile literature. [1. Neck. 2. Shoulder. 3. Human anatomy.] I. Title. II. Series.
   QM535 .S3553 2003
   612'.93–dc21

                              2002014741

Acknowledgments
The author and publishers are grateful to the following for permission to reproduce copyright material:
p. 4 George Shelley/Corbis; pp. 5, 6, 8, 9T, 14, 17, 21, 22 Brian Warling/Heinemann Library; p. 7 Robert Lifson/Heinemann Library; p. 9B Chris Cole/All Sport/Getty Images; p. 10 Benedet/PhotoTake; p. 12 Bob Daemmrich/Stock Boston, Inc./PictureQuest; p. 13 Jeff Greenberg/PhotoEdit; p. 15 Alan Jakubek/Corbis; p. 16 Ken Kaminesky/Corbis; p. 18 CNRI/PhotoTake; p. 20 Tom & Dee Ann McCarthy/Corbis; p. 23 Custom Medical Stock Photo; back cover Custom Medical Stock Photo

Cover photograph by David Stoecklein/Corbis

Every effort has been made to contact copyright holders of any material reproduced in this book. Any omissions will be rectified in subsequent printings if notice is given to the publisher.

Special thanks to our advisory panel for their help in the preparation of this book:

Alice Bethke, Library Consultant
Palo Alto, CA

Eileen Day, Preschool Teacher
Chicago, IL

Kathleen Gilbert,
Second Grade Teacher
Round Rock, TX

Sandra Gilbert,
Library Media Specialist
Fiest Elementary School
Houston, TX

Jan Gobeille,
Kindergarten Teacher
Garfield Elementary
Oakland, CA

Angela Leeper,
Educational Consultant
North Carolina Department
of Public Instruction
Wake Forest, NC

Some words are shown in bold, **like this.**
You can find them in the picture glossary on page 23.

Contents

What Are Your Neck and Shoulders?

Your neck and shoulders are parts of your body.

Your body is made up of many parts.

Your neck and shoulders are **joints.**

Joints help you move your body.

Where Is Your Neck?

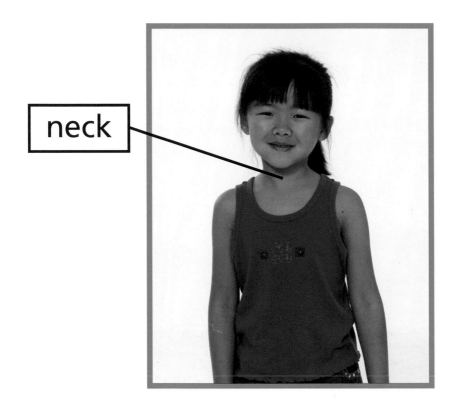

neck

Your neck is between your shoulders.

Your neck joins your head to your body.

The neck **joint** helps your head move.

Your head can move left, right, up, and down.

What Does Your Neck Look Like?

Your neck is shaped like a **tube**.

It is covered with smooth skin.

Some necks are long and thin.

Other necks are short and thick.

What Is Inside Your Neck?

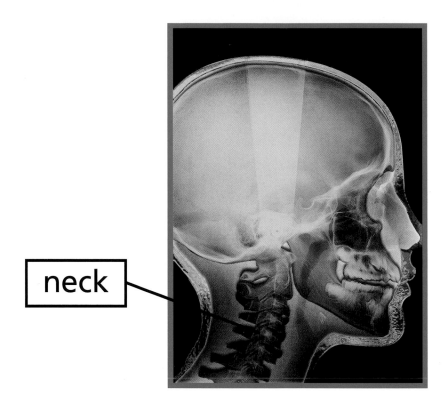

neck

Muscles and **bones** are inside your neck.

Muscles help your bones move.

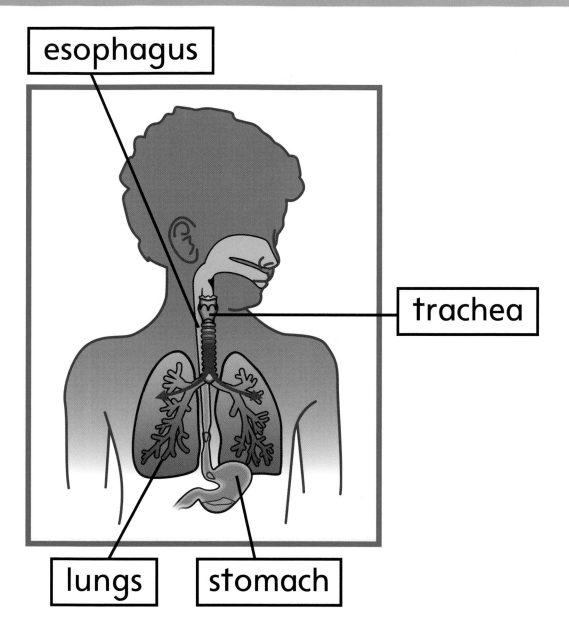

esophagus

trachea

lungs

stomach

The **esophagus** in your neck takes food to your **stomach.**

The **trachea** takes air to your **lungs.**

What Can You Do with Your Neck?

Your neck helps you nod yes or no.

It helps you look left and right.

Your neck helps you look up at the sky.

It helps you look down at your feet.

Where Are Your Shoulders?

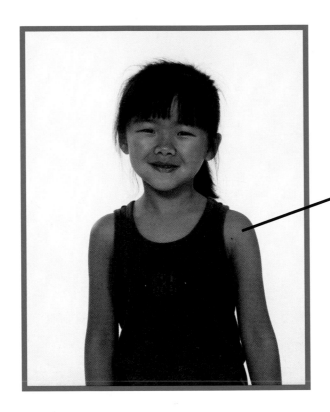

shoulders

Your shoulders are at the tops of your arms.

You have two shoulders.

Shoulders join your arms to your body.

Shoulder **joints** help your arms move.

What Do Your Shoulders Look Like?

Shoulders look round.

They are covered with smooth skin.

Grown-ups have big shoulders.

Babies have little shoulders.

What Is Inside Your Shoulders?

shoulder bone

arm bone

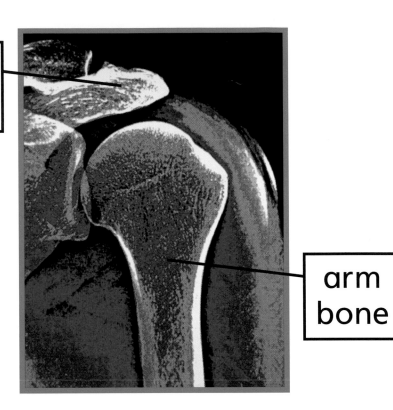

Bones are inside your shoulders.

The arm bone fits in the shoulder bone.

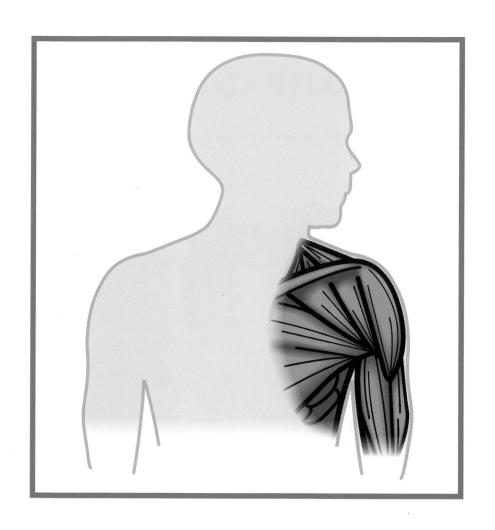

Muscles are inside your shoulders.

Muscles help your bones move.

What Can You Do with Your Shoulders?

Your shoulders help you reach high.

Your shoulders can show that
you don't know.

Quiz

Can you guess what these are?

Look for the answers on page 24.

?

?

Picture Glossary

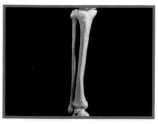

bone
pages 10, 18, 19

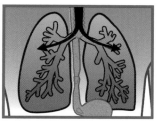

lungs
page 11

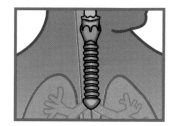

trachea
(TRAY-kee-ya)
page 11

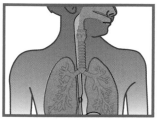

esophagus
(uh-SOF-uh-gus)
page 11

muscle
pages 10, 19

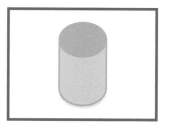

tube
page 8

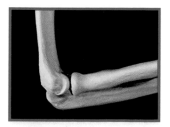

joint
pages 5, 7, 15

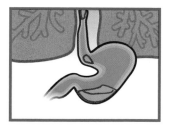

stomach
page 11

Note to Parents and Teachers

Reading for information is an important part of a child's literacy development. Learning begins with a question about something. Help children think of themselves as investigators and researchers by encouraging their questions about the world around them. Each chapter in this book begins with a question. Read the question together. Look at the pictures. Talk about what you think the answer might be. Then read the text to find out if your predictions were correct. Think of other questions you could ask about the topic, and discuss where you might find the answers. Assist children in using the picture glossary and the index to practice new vocabulary and research skills.

Index

Answers to quiz on page 22

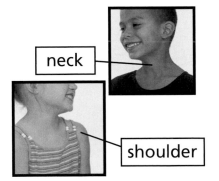

neck

shoulder

24